POSTAL WORKERS

A TO Z

Text and Photographs
Jean Johnson

Walker and Company
New York

Acknowledgments:

In addition to the U.S. Postal Service employees in Charlotte, N.C., I would like to thank the postal workers in Davidson, N.C., Cramerton, N.C., Bowling Green, S.C., and Sun City, Ariz. for their help. I would also like to thank my father, J. C. Pinkerton, for his contribution.

First published in the United States of America in 1987 by the Walker Publishing Company, Inc.

Published simultaneously in Canada by Beaverbooks, Limited, Pickering, Ontario.

Library of Congress Cataloging-in-Publication Data

Johnson, Jean, 1943–
    Postal workers, A to Z.

    (Community helpers series)
    1. Postal service—United
States—Employees—Juvenile
literature.   2. Postal service—United States—Juvenile
literature.   I. Title.   II. Series: Community helpers
series (New York, N.Y.)
HE6499.J64   1987   383′.145′02373   86-11089
ISBN 0-8027-6663-3
ISBN 0-8027-6664-1 (lib. bdg.)

Printed in the United States of America

10 9 8 7 6 5 4 3 2 1

Book design by Laurie McBarnette

To the U.S. Postal Service employees of
Charlotte, North Carolina,
whose support and
cooperation made this book
possible.

A
Address

The address on this valentine tells postal workers where to send it. An address tells who the letter is going to, where the person lives, and the ZIP Code.

J. Pinkerton
931 N Waiola
Charlotte, N.C. 28203

Mr. S.A. Posten
1127 Dormont St.
Star, WV 26505

LOVE LOVE LOVE
USA 22 USA 22 USA 22

B
Boxes

This child is mailing a letter by putting it in a special box that says U.S. Mail.

Postal workers pick up the mail from boxes almost every day. They load it into their trucks and take it to the post office.

Clerks

These postal workers are called clerks. Some clerks work at the counter in the front of the post office. The counter is like a store. The clerks sell stamps and weigh packages.

Other clerks sort mail at the back of the post office. Each little box holds mail for a different route or part of town. The clerk reads the address and puts the letter in the right box.

D
Dock

At the post office dock, mail trucks are loaded and unloaded. The truck driver and mail handler are taking mail off the truck and into the post office. The dock is covered to protect the mail from rain and snow.

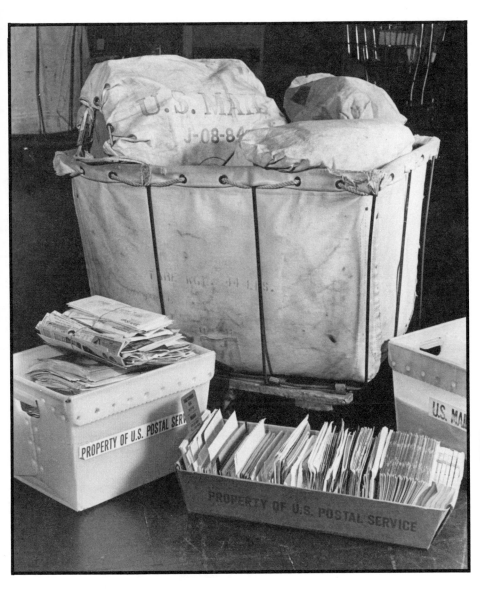

E
Equipment

Postal workers use this equipment to move the mail around. Trays hold letters. Boxes are for large envelopes and ads. Large hampers on wheels are used for moving big loads of mail. The canvas bags in the hamper can be filled with mail, closed, and locked.

F

Facer–Canceller

Postal workers at a big post office use the facer-canceller machine to print postmarks on envelopes. The machine turns letters so they all face the same way. It cancels the stamp so it can't be used again by printing words or wavy lines over it. A postmark is printed to show when and where the letter was mailed.

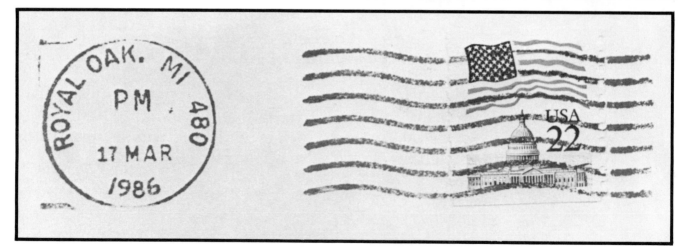

G
Garage

The post office has special garages for repairing mail trucks. Mechanics repair engines, change tires, and check brakes. Drivers use extra mail trucks while theirs are being repaired.

9

H
Holidays

This postal worker is delivering holiday packages. People send lots of extra letters, cards, and packages on holidays. Christmas, Valentine's Day, and Mother's Day are the busiest times of year for the post office.

10

Ink Pad and Stamps

Postal clerks use ink pads and stamps to put words on packages and letters. Stamping the words is quick and the permanent ink won't rub off. The stamps say things such as "first class" and "special delivery." Sometimes they show the postmark.

J Jet Airplanes

Jet airplanes carry lots of mail. Traveling by jet is the fastest way mail can move. Mailbags are loaded into the baggage compartment.

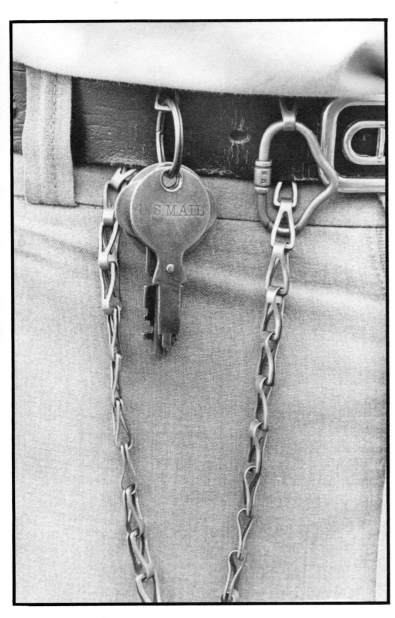

K
Keys

Letter carriers carry keys on a long chain so they can open mailboxes. The collection boxes are kept locked to protect the mail. Postal workers are the only people allowed to take mail out of a box.

Letter Carrier

This letter carrier is at the post office sorting the mail she will deliver. She puts together all the mail going to the same address. There is a slot for every address.

When the carrier has finished sorting, she delivers the mail. She reads the house number and puts all the mail for that house in its mailbox.

M Mail

You can send different kinds of things in the mail. The post office delivers letters, magazines, newspapers, ads, and packages.

N

Night

These postal workers are going into a large post office to work at night. They will sort mail, run machines, and load trucks. This work is done at night so the mail can be delivered during the day.

Office Mail

Postal workers handle more office mail than any other kind of mail. Letter carriers often walk into business offices to deliver the mail.

P

Postage Stamps

You buy postage stamps to pay for sending your mail. Stamps have different prices because some mail costs more to send. There are many interesting pictures on stamps. A lot of people like to collect different kinds of stamps.

Q

Quick Service

You get quick service when you use Express Mail. Mail sent this way arrives the same day or overnight, no matter where it is going. It travels in specially marked boxes and envelopes so that postal workers will know they should handle it quickly.

R Rural Carriers

Rural carriers deliver most of their mail in the country. They sort their mail at the post office. Then they drive their own cars and put the mail in boxes along the road. Rural carriers also sell stamps, mail packages, and offer many of the same services as post offices.

S
Scales

Postal clerks weigh mail on scales to find out how much it will cost to send. The heavier the mail, the more postage it will need.

T
Trucks

The post office uses many trucks to move the mail. Large trucks go to the airport, nearby towns, and the big post offices. Small trucks collect letters from mailboxes and pick up mail at the local post office.

27

28

U

U.S. Post Office

There are U.S. Post Offices all over the United States, in small towns and big cities. The post office is for everyone in the nation. There is an American flag in front of most post offices.

V
Vehicles

These vehicles help letter carriers deliver the mail. The post office rents small cars for some carriers. Mail jeeps with right-hand drive allow letter carriers to deliver from the driver's window. Carriers even use bicycles.

W

Wrong Address

This clerk is stamping mail that has the wrong address. Postal workers have already tried to deliver this mail. Mail that cannot be delivered because of a wrong address is stamped with a picture of a hand and returned to the sender.

X-Ray

Sometimes postal inspectors X-ray the inside of a package they think might be dangerous. It is against the law to mail things that might seriously hurt someone. Postal inspectors protect us from people who misuse the mail. However, they are not allowed to open mail without a search warrant.

Y

Year–Round

Letter carriers work outside year-round and must be prepared for heat in summer and cold in winter. They have shorts for hot weather, rain gear and rubbers for rainy days, and heavy jackets, warm hats, and gloves for cold days. The mail is always delivered, even in the worst weather.

Z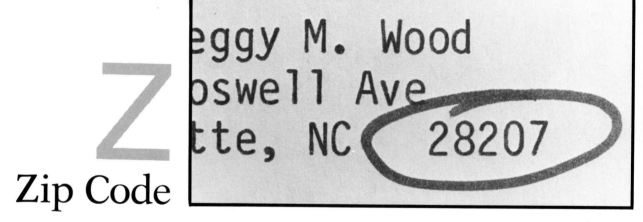

Zip Code

ZIP Codes are numbers that tell which state and city you live in. This clerk is using a computerized machine that sorts the mail by ZIP Code. It is very important to use the right ZIP Code on your letter.

More About Postal Workers and the Post Office

In this section, many postal procedures are described
in greater detail to increase awareness
of the importance to our communities of the post office and its workers
and to enhance classroom discussion.

The United States Postal Service is a complex organization. It is a giant network of postal workers, machines, and trucks that operates around the clock to sort, process, and distribute the mail. Besides local post offices, it also has sectional mail processing centers that serve large geographical areas. Almost all mail goes through a sectional center and then a local post office.

Your local post office is a busy place. At the front of the building inside there is a retail counter. Here clerks weigh mail and sell stamps, pre-stamped postcards and envelopes, money orders, and package insurance. Many post offices also issue food stamps and take passport applications.

The clerk helps you decide the best way to send your mail. There are several special mail services available for extra fees besides Express Mail. Valuables may be sent by registered mail. These items are kept safe in a fenced, locked area of the post office until they are delivered. Certified mail travels with regular mail, but must be signed for. And COD (Collect On Delivery) allows a person to pay for an item at the time it is delivered. Special delivery mail is delivered by a carrier soon after it arrives at the destination post office.

At the counter, you can arrange to rent an individual mailbox. These are usually located in a separate lobby or hallway that is open even when the post office is closed. Customers renting these boxes have a key which allows them to pick up their mail any time day or night.

Clerks who work at the retail counter keep careful records of the items they sell and the money they collect. Stamps and cash are kept in a locked safe when the counter is not open. Money collected at the counter supports the U.S. Postal Service, a non-profit, independent government agency.

The back of a local post office is a work room. Mail from the sectional center begins to arrive as early as 3:00 A.M. It is processed and partially sorted. Clerks distribute box mail and give the carriers their mail for the day. On an average route, letter carriers deliver two thousand pieces of mail a day and travel seven or eight miles on foot. Rural carriers average sixty miles a day and six hundred deliveries. Most post offices close at 5:00 P.M. In a large city post office, however, some clerks work night shifts sorting mail for delivery the next day.

Meanwhile, the sectional center is preparing for its most active time of day. By 5:00 P.M. mail has begun to pour in. Trucks bring mail from the city boxes and the airport. Drivers unload the trucks, and mail handlers push hampers, carts, and racks of mail into the building. Inside, mail handlers empty bags of mail onto conveyor belts. Clerks separate packages by destination. Letters are sorted by size and sent to the facer-canceller. This machine locates the stamp, turning the letter over if necessary, cancels the stamp, and puts a postmark on the letter. The postmark shows the date, A.M. or P.M., the city and state, and the first three letters of the ZIP Code. A facer-canceller machine processes about four hundred letters a minute. This mail is then loaded into trays or boxes to be sorted by ZIP Code.

POSTAL SERVICE

S. INTERSTATE 85

LOTTE NC   28228-9998

ZIP Code (Zone Improvement Program) reduces the cost of mailing letters by speeding up sorting. The first three letters of a ZIP Code identify the section of the country and the state. The last two numbers direct the mail to a delivering post office. The addition of ZIP + 4 (used primarily by large businesses) makes it possible for mail to be directed to a street or specific block area. The optical character reader and the bar code sorter are two automated machines used to sort the mail by ZIP Code. The optical character reader scans the address, applies the bar code (hatch marks), and automatically sends the letter into the chute for that ZIP Code. These machines can process five hundred letters a minute. Present scanners cannot read handwritten ZIP Codes. Mail rejected for this reason is sent to the letter-sorting machine to have the ZIP Code typed into a computer by a clerk.

Mail is dispatched throughout the night. Mail trucks deliver to airports, stations, and nearby cities. Independent highway contractors carry mail to distant cities and distribution centers. The airlines carry a high percentage of first class, Express, and registered mail. The sectional centers process mail twenty-four hours a day, every day of the year.

tte, N.C. 28203

The Postal Inspection Service, a federal law enforcement agency, watches over all the postal workers and operations at sectional centers and post offices. It provides physical security for the mail, employees, and postal property. Its trained officers investigate crimes such as mail fraud, stolen mail, and bombs or illegal drugs sent in the mail. Postal inspectors carry guns and wear badges. They work closely with all other federal law enforcement agencies and with the local police.

The postal service offers us an inexpensive, dependable way to communicate. Postal workers take great pride in their jobs and in the quality of service they offer. They sort, process, and deliver billions of pieces of mail each year with a low percentage of error. Through the mail, we can exchange news, ideas, and knowledge with anyone in the world. Our communities, both rural and urban, depend upon postal workers to bring mail that keeps us informed and enriches our lives.

Other Titles in the Community Helpers Series

FIRE FIGHTERS
A TO Z

POLICE OFFICERS
A TO Z

COPY 1

Johnson, Jean

Postal workers A to Z

DISCARD

DATE			

© THE BAKER & TAYLOR CO.